D0959797

9-EAT-676

Dear .... ,

Dear Graduate

by Charles McEnerney + Adam Larson

Adam&Co.

First Edition, March 2022
Copyright © 2022 Charles McEnerney and Adam Larson
All rights reserved.

Published in the United States by Adam&Co.
279 Chestnut Ave #1, Jamaica Plain, MA 02130

ISBN: 978-0-578-36423-0

To purchase hardcover or ebook versions,
visit **deargraduatebook.com.**

For bookstore sales or bulk orders email
deargraduatebook@gmail.com or call/text (617) 233-6613

Printed in Braintree, Massachusetts.

For Adacie & Declan

A book for when we take a step forward.

When we are young,
we are often asked
the question...

What do you
want to be
when you
grow up?

A difficult question—
and how is one to
know?

But what if the question wasn't, "What do you want to be?"

What if
we asked...

What will you
do when you
grow up?

Will you design and build the structures that keep us safe and warm inside?

Will you sow seeds
and grow and
harvest us healthy
things to eat?

Will you care for our health, our bodies, minds, and souls?

Will you transform numbers and letters and symbols into code?

Will you invent
something useful
that we've never
seen before?

Will you grow
flowers or bring
them and joy to
our doors?

Will you drive trucks and buses and move mountains, people, and everything we need?

Will you juggle
numbers, dishes, or
bowling ball pins?

Will you stay
with your children,
to raise them and
teach them?

Will you care for
the babies, toddlers,
and children of those
at work?

Will you rescue someone when they are in trouble?

Will you engineer and build bikes or cars or ships or space stations?

Will you measure, stir, and bake or prep, cook, and clean?

Will you hit, throw, or bat or swim, lift, or ski?

Will you help manage the power of our water, energy, or electricity?

Will you sing, dance, act, or create to bring beauty, emotion, and truth to our days?

Will you teach, to inspire, nurture, and share your knowledge?

Will you honor your elders, who have lived life well and shared their wisdom with you?

Will you make a plan to contribute to a better world, to improve it for others?

Will you look toward the future, and take risks or chances and challenge yourself?

Will you cheer on your friends and family to succeed?

Will you mentor someone younger, offering guidance when they need it most?

Will you treat every other person, animal, and living thing with respect and care?

Will you remember those who lifted you up and helped you become you?

Will you respect
what others choose
to do, too?

Will you consider
all points of view,
encourage diversity
of thought?

Will you try and see the world, how we each live and breathe?

Will you keep
your mind open,
listen and learn to
understand others?

Will you keep your mind open, learn something new every day?

No matter
what you do,
my wish
for you...

is that you
find dignity,

pride in all
of your
accomplishments,

and satisfaction
your whole life
through.

Congratulations!

Charles McEnerney

Charles McEnerney is a writer, musician, marketer and, most importantly, a dad to Adacie and Declan. He helped people be entertained while working at HBO, *MovieMaker* Magazine, Seattle International Film Festival, *Fast Company* and *Inc.* Magazines, WGBH/PBS, ArtsBoston, Emerson College, and The Grommet. He also hosted and produced the Well-Rounded Radio podcast. He grew up in Flushing, Queens in New York City and currently lives in Jamaica Plain in Boston, Massachusetts. He graduated from PS 21, St. Michael's, Holy Cross High School, and New York University. charlesmcenerney.com

Adam Larson

Adam Larson is an artist, creative director, designer, illustrator, and founder of award-winng brand design studio, Adam&Co. He has created beauty for clients such as Beyoncé, Taylor Swift, Fleetwood Mac, Nike, Puma, Saucony, Converse, The Boston Public Library, The Isabella Stewart Gardner Museum, CNN, Samuel Adams, 2K Sports, Major League Baseball, and hundreds of others. He grew up in Stoneham, Massachusetts and currently lives in Florence, Massachusetts with his American Bully named Rhys. He graduated from Robin Hood Elementary, Stoneham Middle School, Stoneham High School, and Syracuse University. adamnco.com

Thank you to Patricia McEnerney, Marion Seymour, Natalie Jackvony, and Boozies.